THE POCKET SIZE

Student's Companion

Artwork by Linda Ketelhut

RONNIE
SELLERS
PRODUCTIONS
PORTLAND, MAINE

Published by Ronnie Sellers Productions, Inc.
P.O. Box 818, Portland, Maine 04104
For ordering information:
Phone: (800) MAKE-FUN (625-3386)
Fax: (207) 772-6814
Visit our Web site: www.makefun.com
E-mail: rsp@rsvp.com

ISBN: 1-56906-531-4

Printed in China